Published by Creative Education
P.O. Box 227, Mankato, Minnesota 56002
Creative Education is an imprint of
The Creative Company
www.thecreativecompany.us

Design by The Design Lab
Production by Chelsey Luther
Art direction by Rita Marshall
Printed in the United States of America

Photographs by Alamy (Peter Arnold, Inc.), Corbis
(Ron Austing/Frank Lane Picture Agency), Dreamstime
(Joye Ardyn Durham), Getty Images (Roy Toft, James
Warwick, Art Wolfe), iStockphoto (gary forsyth, Laura
Hart, Megan Lorenz, Frank van den Bergh), National
Geographic (JOHN BOOTH/National Geographic
My Shot, MICHAEL S. QUINTON), Shutterstock (Eric
Isselée), SuperStock (All Canada Photos)

Library of Congress Cataloging-in-Publication Data
Bodden, Valerie.
Owls / by Valerie Bodden.
p. cm. — (Amazing animals)
Summary: A basic exploration of the appearance,
behavior, and habitat of owls, the winged nighttime
hunters. Also included is a story from folklore explain-
ing why some owls have big eyes and ears.
Includes bibliographical references and index.
ISBN 978-1-60818-088-2
1. Owls—Juvenile literature. I. Title.
QL696.S83B63 2013
598.9'7—dc23   2011050280

First Edition
9 8 7 6 5 4 3 2 1

AMAZING ANIMALS

OWLS

BY VALERIE BODDEN

CREATIVE EDUCATION

Barn owls are found in places all around the world

An owl is a **bird of prey**. There are more than 200 kinds of owls in the world. They are split into two families. Barn owls have a heart-shaped face. Typical owls come in many different shapes and sizes.

bird of prey a bird that hunts and eats other animals

Owls

are covered with brown, gray, reddish, or white feathers. They have large heads with big eyes and hooked beaks. They have long wings and sharp toenails called talons, too. Some owls also have large tufts of feathers that look like ears.

The great horned owl has large ear tufts on its head

The smallest owls are less than 5.5 inches (14 cm) long. The biggest owls can weigh as much as a newborn human baby. They can be 28 inches (70 cm) long. Some owls' wings stretch more than six feet (1.8 m) across!

The Eastern screech owl (above) is smaller than the great gray owl (opposite)

Owls live everywhere on Earth except Antarctica. Some owls live in forests. Others live in dry, hot deserts or in grasslands.

Some owls make nests inside desert plants called cacti

Owls eat small animals such as mice. Some eat birds or insects. Owls swallow their food without chewing it. Later, they spit out feathers, fur, and bones.

Owls catch food and bring it back to their young

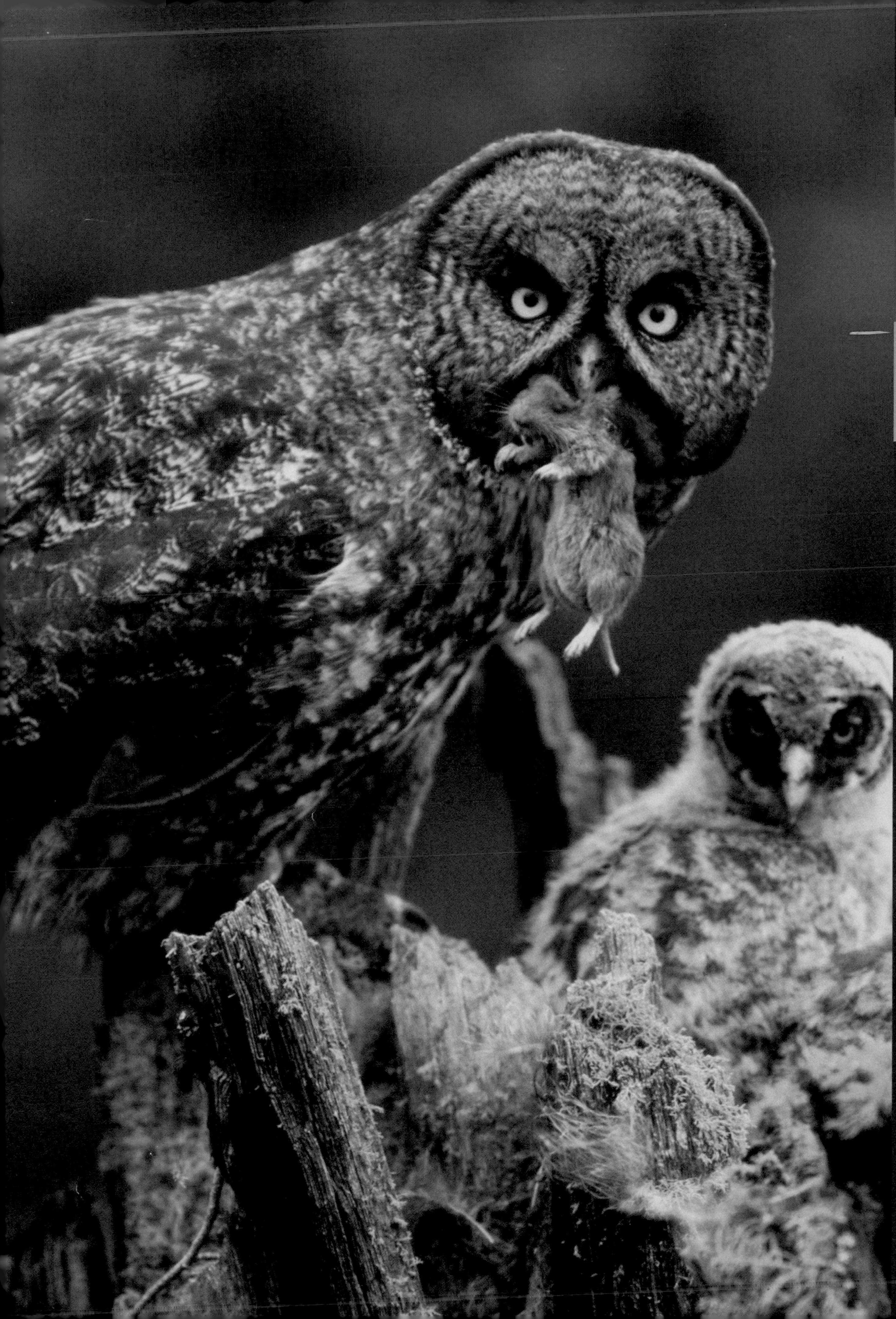

Owlets lose their down feathers as they get older

Female owls lay 2 to 12 eggs. When **owlets** are born, they are covered with soft feathers called down. Owlets leave their mother after about five months. Young owls have to watch out for larger birds that might eat them. But grown owls have few **predators**. They can live 20 years in the wild.

owlets baby owls

predators animals that kill and eat other animals

Owls like to sleep when they are not hunting

Most owls sleep during the day and are active at night. They often sit on a tree branch until they see or hear **prey**. Then they dive down and catch it.

OWLS

prey animals that are killed and eaten by other animals

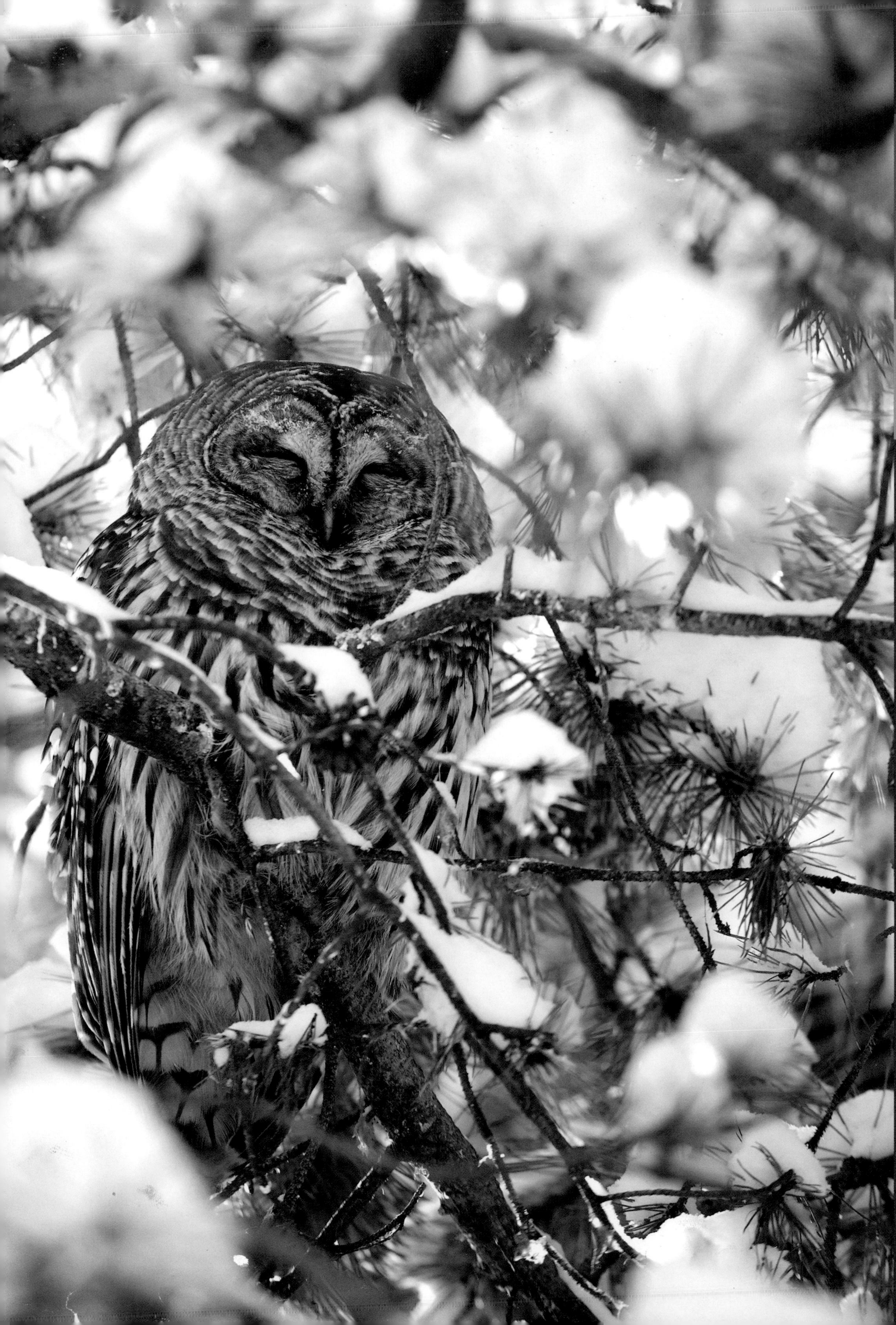

Owls make many kinds of sounds. Some hoot. Others chirp, whistle, or sing. They also make sounds by snapping their beaks and clapping their wings.

Owlets may chirp to get their mother's attention

Owls can be hard to find in the wild because they sleep during the day. But some people like to search for them. Others set up boxes for owls to nest in. And many people see owls in zoos. It can be fun to see these nighttime birds up-close!

*The colors of some owls'
feathers help them hide*

Why do some owls have big eyes and ear tufts? **American Indians** used to tell a story about this. When the creator made animals, he let them choose how they wanted to look. He told Owl not to watch him make the other animals. But Owl watched anyway. As a result, the creator pulled on Owl's ear feathers. Owl's eyes got big with fear. So now many owls have large eyes and ear tufts!

American Indians the first people to live in North America before white people came

Read More

Morgan, Sally. *Owls*. Laguna Hills, Calif.: QEB Publishing, 2006.

Schuetz, Kari. *Owls*. Minneapolis: Bellwether Media, 2012.

Snedden, Robert. *Bird*. North Mankato, Minn.: Smart Apple Media, 2008.

Web Sites

National Geographic Kids Creature Features: Snowy Owls
http://kids.nationalgeographic.com/kids/animals/creaturefeature/snowy-owl/
This site has facts, pictures, and videos of snowy owls.

The Owl Pages
http://www.owlpages.com/
This site has pictures of owls, and you can also listen to different owl sounds.

Index